THE FAMILY CIRCUS® IS

VERY KEANE

Bil Keane

Fawcett Columbine • New York

Here is black and white proof of why The Family Circus is Very Keane. In 1960, the year the feature was introduced to newspaper readers across America, the Keanes had this family portrait taken in Phoenix, Arizona. Along with Thel, recognizable as Mommy, are the other models for the cartoons.

From left in front are Glen, Jeff and Chris. Standing: Gayle (nicknamed Dolly when she was tiny) and Neal. On the last page of this book you'll find a cartoonist's update of the family as they are today.

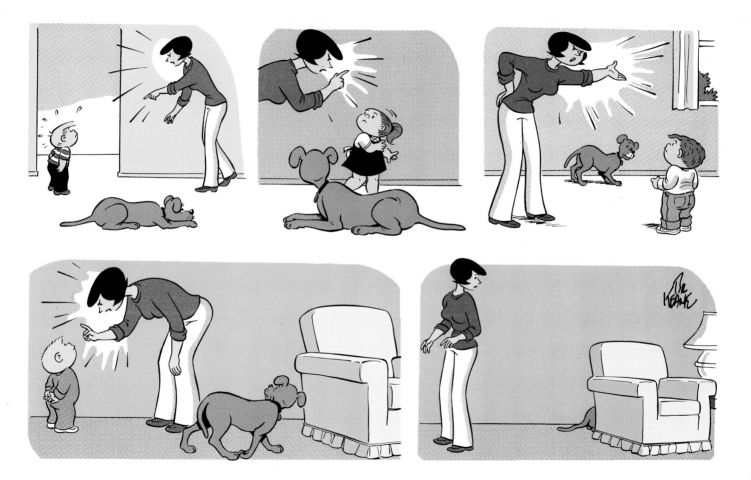

Sun and Dotter

This Bear's Repeating

Ill Eagle N Tree

Chuting a Basket

Condescending

OLYMPICS AROUND HOME

DISCUS THROW

FENCING

COMPULSORY EXERCISES

TOYS

100 M BUTTERFLY

HAMMER THROW

SHOOTING

WEIGHT LIFTING

SOCCER!

TRACK

BIL KEANE

CLOSING CEREMONIES

WATER SPORTS

HURDLES

DID THEY HAVE THE OLYMPICS WHEN YOU WERE YOUNG, DADDY?
I LIKE THAT MUSIC THEY'RE PLAYIN', BUT I DON'T KNOW THE WORDS TO IT.
KNOW WHY THEY CALL 'EM "HURDLES"? IF YOU TRIP IT'LL HURDLE LOT!

WHILE BIL KEANE TAKES A WEEK'S VACATION, 7 YEAR OLD BILLY TAKES OVER THE DRAWING BOARD TO PROVIDE THESE CHILD'S-EYE OBSERVATIONS.

Coffee has magic in it. Daddy can't smile in the morning till after he has some.

The softest, warmest pillows in the whole world are dogs.

Here's some bread, birds! Come back here!

Birds don't like company when they're eating.

Cats must be dumb. They wash their hands when nobody told them to.

OOPS.

If the yellow part breaks when Mommy's getting an egg out of the pan it's always hers.

Hi, Mr. Warner, Hello Mr. Miller...

The first name of most of Daddy's friends is "Mister."

You can tell it's
Friday when Daddy
comes home from
work whistling

Grandmas are mommies
with lots of practice.

Crying is a
waste of time
if Mommy
can't hear you.

The favorite time for
fathers to do things
is "later".

TO HELP BIL KEANE CELEBRATE HIS BIRTHDAY THIS WEEKEND BILLY CONTRIBUTES THIS NEW EDITION OF HIS SPECIAL MAP.
Map # 3 By Billy (age 7)
Oh-Pun Country
Notta Sound
Boy Gorge
Cart Ridge
Silkwood
Cherry Pitts
George Bush
Gar Field
Mary Tyler Moor
Savings Bank
Ethel Waters
Strike It Ridge
Mount To-Somethin'
Peter Paul Mounds
True-or Falls
Box Springs
M & M's Plain
Collie Flower
Eye Land
Mark Trail
Jeff Bridges
Rock of Ages
Amster Dam
Ides of Marsh
Gerald Fjord
Ms Tree
Pencil Point
Well Well Well
Stand Up Strait!
Lepro-Sea
Ray Window
Palm Reading

RUNNING HARD TO WIN

FACING THE ISSUES

CAMPAIGN PROMISES

CONTRIBUTING TO THE PARTY

APPEALING TO A MINORITY GROUP

SUPPORTING A FAVORITE SON

A REAL UPSET

TV DEBATE

MAKING A CONCESSION SPEECH

Now grown, Bil Keane's models are all residents of California. Jeff is an aspiring actor in Los Angeles and assistant to his dad; Chris is a marine biologist and research scientist in Santa Cruz; Glen is an animator at Walt Disney Studios and author/illustrator of children's books; Neal is a computer design engineer and musician in Panorama City; Gayle operates her own flower and plant shop (BloominGayle's) in Sacramento.

At his drawing board in Paradise Valley, Arizona, Dad still sees them all as chubby, round-faced, lovable tykes—another reason why The Family Circus is Very Keane.